FRAN TARKENTON
SCRAMBLING QUARTERBACK

FRAN TARKENTON
SCRAMBLING QUARTERBACK

by Julian May

Published by Crestwood House, Inc., Mankato, Minnesota 56001. Text copyright © 1973 by Julian May Dikty. Illustrations copyright © 1973 by Crestwood House, Inc. All rights reserved. No part of this book may be reproduced in any form without written permission from the publisher, except for brief passages included in a review. Printed in the United States of America.

Reprinted 1978

Designed by William Dichtl   Revised 1977

Library of Congress Catalog Card Number: 73-80423

International Standard Book Numbers:
0-913940-03-8 Library Bound
0-913940-96-8 Paperback

Crestwood House, Inc., Mankato, Minn. 56001

PHOTOGRAPHIC CREDITS

Wide World: 6, 30, 35; The Trojan (courtesy of Louise Chandler and Ruby Anderson): 8-9, 10, 11, 12; University of Georgia: 13, 14, 15, 16-17; United Press International: 19, 24-25, 26, 28, 29, 31, 32, 33, 34, 38, 40, 41, 44-45, 47; Minneapolis Star: 20, 21, 22-23; National Football League: 27 (John E. Martin) 36-37 (Russ Russell); Crestwood House, Inc.: 29; Vernon J. Biever: 43, 46

FRAN TARKENTON
SCRAMBLING QUARTERBACK

He was a minister's boy.

For his first ten years he was small for his age. He had asthma, which sometimes made it hard for him to breathe. But that didn't stop him from playing on a boys' club football team in his home city of Washington, D.C.

When he wasn't on the field, he was in his bedroom, planning make-believe games. His team was the 1950 Philadelphia Eagles—on bubble-gum cards.

And he, Francis Tarkenton, was always the quarterback.

"Someday," he told himself, "I'll play quarterback in Yankee Stadium in New York. The whole world will cheer."

The Tarkenton family was very religious. But Fran's father did not worry about his son's interest in sports.

"God inspired me to become a pastor," he said to his son. "He may inspire you to become an athlete."

"I hope so!" said young Fran.

The family moved to Athens, Georgia, the next year. There were many good sports opportunities for boys. Fran began to grow tall and strong. He played football and basketball, and he was a star Little League Baseball pitcher. In 1952, Fran helped his Little League team win the city championship.

He entered Athens High the next year and was a good student. Sports were still the center of his life, however. Even as a freshman, he made the varsity teams in football, baseball, and basketball.

He liked baseball best. In 1954, he hit .365 and helped bring the team to the regional championships. There he struck out 26 men in 22 innings and batted .417. The team won the title after Fran pitched a one-hitter.

The 1954 Athens Trojans featured two Tarkentons. Fran *(10)* was rookie quarterback; his older brother Dallas *(20)* played fullback. At far right, Coach Weyman Sellers.

Fran played guard on the Athens basketball team.

That fall, he went out for football again. As a frosh quarterback, he had spent most of his time studying the game. Now he was ready to win. Athens High took nine games out of ten that year. Then they met Rockmart for the playoff that would decide the North Georgia title.

With Fran Tarkenton as quarterback, the Athens squad dominated the game. The score was tied, 6-6, in the last minutes. According to the rules, Athens was about to be declared winner on a technicality.

But this wasn't good enough for Fran. He decided to gamble on his team's ability to score again. He called a rollout pass to the right and threw.

The ball was intercepted. A Rockmart player ran away with it for a touchdown.

Fran's gamble had lost his team the regional title. Some of the boys wept in the locker room. But Fran said:

"We'll whip 'em next time."

Fran was active in many high-school organizations. Here he presides as president of the Student-Faculty Cooperative Association.

Fran's first love was still baseball. He dreamed of becoming a major league pitcher. During the 1955 season, the Athens team was doing well and Fran was the star hurler.

Then they met Covington, a tough team to beat. Fran, standing out on the mound, studied the heavy hitter who was next up to bat. He thought, "I'll give the ball a little extra spin this time."

He wound up and threw. There was a sudden *snap!* The pitch went wild and Fran's arm exploded in pain. He had torn a tendon below the elbow. When it healed, he found that his pitching ability was gone forever.

Much later, Fran would consider the accident a lucky one. It turned his attention from baseball to football, because strangely enough, he could throw a pass as well as ever.

He proved this in the fall opener of his junior year. Fran threw two touchdown passes and Athens won. They took the next nine games, too. It seemed nothing could stop them. Again they met Rockmart for the playoff, but this time Athens was the winner by a healthy 26-7 score. Then it was time to face powerful Valdosta for the state championship. The underdog Athens team amazed everyone by whipping Valdosta, 41-20.

During that great 1955 season, Fran proved himself an outstanding quarterback. Not only could he pass, but he could also run. Often, when his receivers were not in position, he would dash around to escape opposing linemen instead of staying in the traditional "pocket."

When Fran graduated from Athens High in 1957, he had 50 scholarship offers. But he had already made up his mind to attend the University of Georgia in his own home city.

Three co-captains of the 1957 Athens Trojans pose together. *(Left to right)* Coach Harry Hamilton, Ronnie Bond, Fran Tarkenton, Doug Ross, Coach Weyman Sellers.

Georgia's veteran football coach, Wally Butts, needed new talent. His Bulldogs had had two losing seasons. They were headed for the third in a row in 1957.

The future looked brighter to Coach Butts as he watched the freshman squad. Led by quarterback Fran Tarkenton, the frosh were unbeaten and untied for the first time in 20 years.

In 1958, Fran joined the varsity as a third-string quarterback. In the first game, against Texas, Georgia trailed 7-0 in the last quarter. Coach Butts sent Fran in. He sparked a 95-yard drive that led to a touchdown and a two-point conversion.

Coach Wally Butts of the University of Georgia.

Four Athens boys pose with Coach Butts. *(Left to right)* Bobby Towns, Fran Tarkenton, Billy Slaughter, George Guisler.

But the coach was cautious with rookies. He benched Fran and sent in another quarterback. In the last minutes, Texas scored again and won the game.

For the rest of his sophomore year, Fran saw little real action. The Bulldogs lost six games out of ten. They went into the 1959 season as underdogs. Fran and senior Charley Britt shared the quarterbacking.

In the first game, Georgia faced mighty Alabama. No one expected much from the Bulldogs. But Fran fooled them all, leading his team to a 17-3 upset.

14

Fran and his fiancee, drum marjorette Elaine Merrell, after a game with Georgia Tech.

The next game saw the team in Tennessee challenging Vanderbilt. Fran made good on six of seven passes. The team won, 21-6, and Fran had been responsible for two of the touchdowns.

Feeling cocky, the Bulldogs went after South Carolina. Fran completed 14 out of 19 passes, but his receivers fumbled four times. Georgia lost, 30-14. Old Wally Butts brought his men back under control and the Bulldogs marched on, taking the next five games. For the first time in years, the Bulldogs were a Southeastern Conference threat.

Fran throws the winning TD pass to Billy Herron in the 1959 game against Auburn.

16

The game that would decide the championship was played against Auburn. It was a seesaw battle all the way, but the last two minutes of play saw Georgia trailing, 13-7. Auburn tried to stall. But Pat Dye, Georgia's All-American guard, recovered a fumble on the Auburn 35.

Fran gave everything he had. They drove down to the 13-yard line, fighting hard, while the 55,000 fans pleaded for victory.

With 30 seconds and fourth down to go, Fran called time out. He did an amazing thing. Walking away from the huddle, he closed his eyes and asked God to help him think. When he returned to his men, he had a new play all ready.

He faked a handoff to the fullback and fooled the Auburn defense. Fran rolled out to his right and saw end Billy Herron break free into the end zone.

A soft pass spiraled cross-field into Herron's arms. Fans howled with joy and the score was tied. The converting kick sailed between the posts and Georgia won, 14-13.

The Bulldogs were Conference champions. They went to the Orange Bowl and beat Missouri, 14-0. They were a top team for the first time in 20 years.

But the following year, even though Fran was better than ever, the Bulldogs went into a downhill slide. Too many of the top men had graduated. Georgia wound up the 1960 season with six wins and four losses. Fran's season had been his best, according to the numbers. Late in December, he married his college sweetheart, Elaine Merrell. She had been a drum majorette with the Bulldog band.

Fran had majored in business administration and earned good grades. But he really wanted a career in pro football.

The scouts noticed him, of course. But some shook their heads over his asthma and others remembered his long-ago arm injury. One coach even said that a minister's son would be too "nice" to quarterback a gang of mean, ugly pros.

Still, Fran got letters from the professional teams. One was unusual, from a brand-new team that had been created when the NFL expanded.

Fran asked a friend, "Who are the Minnesota Vikings?"

He would soon find out. They drafted him—on the third round.

His feelings were hurt that he had not been a first-round choice. But he was determined to do his best for the new team. The Viking head coach was Norm Van Brocklin, who had been a great "pocket" quarterback with the Los Angeles Rams and the Philadelphia Eagles. He had led the Eagles to the NFL championship in 1960. Only 36, he was the youngest NFL coach—called upon to build a new team from scratch.

Van Brocklin told Fran: "You won't have a lot to do at first. George Shaw will be starting quarterback. We'll play him and let you learn your trade—nice and slow."

Fran didn't like that one bit. He felt he was ready to play in the pros right away.

Coach Norm Van Brocklin with rookie quarterback Fran Tarkenton.

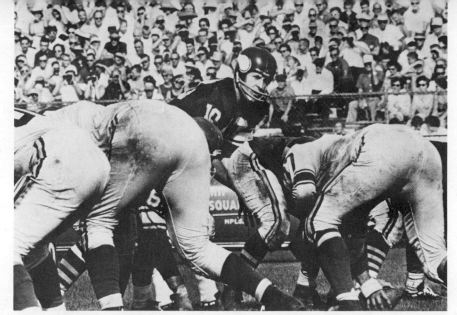
Fran probes the defense in a typical guessing game on the line of scrimmage.

The Vikings' first exhibition games helped teach Fran a lot. He had to unlearn his college tactics and learn the complex patterns of professional football. He found out what a thundering pro defensive line could do to a quarterback whose blockers were still too green to know how to protect him.

In the last exhibition, the Vikings' first home game, Fran faced another kind of challenge. The veteran back, Hugh McElhenny, ran for 50 yards and came back to the huddle panting.

"Kid," he said to Fran, "don't call my play this time. I'm tired!"

McElhenny was a great old player, a man Fran had idolized as a boy. Just the same, Fran called the play again.

Later, McElhenny told the coach: "When that kid called my play a second time. I knew we had a quarterback!"

Hugh McElhenny, from 1952-1960 a back with the San Francisco 49ers, joined the Vikings for two seasons in 1961-1962. He subsequently played for the New York Giants and Detroit Lions.

21

Fran was a quarterback. But there was a more important question still unanswered. Were the Minnesota Vikings a football team? They had lost all five exhibition games, to no one's surprise. For their season opener, they faced the powerful Chicago Bears, the "Monsters of the Midway," who had a reputation for blitzing quarterbacks.

Shaw started. And the surprised and delighted Viking fans saw their new team outplay the visitors. The first quarter gave the Vikings a field goal. Coach Van Brocklin pulled Shaw out and sent in Fran Tarkenton.

Three minutes later, Fran had his first touchdown. He had studied the Bears' defense night and day for a week. And it paid off. In the third quarter, he threw two more touchdown passes. In the fourth he threw a 2-yard pass for another TD, then capped it by running a fifth by himself. The rookie team was doing the impossible.

The Vikings won their first official game, 37-13. They were, indeed, a football team. And Francis Tarkenton was a pro quarterback.

Fran quickly proved himself as a rookie quarterback.

23

The fairy-tale beginning to Fran's career melted away the next week. He did a poor job as they played Dallas and Shaw had to take over. The Vikings lost, 21-7.

The next week, Fran watched from the sidelines. The Vikings battled the mighty Baltimore Colts. With four seconds left, Minnesota led, 33-31. Then Colt Steve Myhra kicked a 52-yard field goal, winning the game.

The broken-hearted team dropped the next four games. Fran played, but did not do very well. He pulled himself together in the eighth game, against Los Angeles. Even though the Vikings lost, Fran completed 12 passes for 156 yards. He also scored with a 52-yard run.

Running around right end, Fran is about to be brought down by George Andrie (66) of the Dallas Cowboys.

Nobody really expects a new team to do well. Still, the Vikings were playing better than fans had a right to hope. If only they had a better defense!

Despite his defeats, Fran was learning fast. He could rarely depend on his blockers. So more often than not he found himself dodging behind the line of scrimmage, searching for a receiver while rival linemen tried to flatten him.

Other teams were baffled by this unusual action. In 1961, nobody expected a pro quarterback to scramble. A few linemen protested that it was illegal! But Fran just couldn't understand why he should stand there and "eat" the ball. If he had the legs and the nerve to scramble, he felt he might still keep the play alive.

Fran scrambles against San Francisco.

In their ninth game, the Vikings faced Baltimore again. Fran started for Minnesota. His opposite number on the Colts was Johnny Unitas.

At the half, the teams were tied 14-14. Baltimore managed a field goal, but the Vikings scored another touchdown, led by Fran.

In the last period, a Colt field goal brought the score to 21-20. Could the Vikings keep their precious one-point lead? Johnny Unitas tried to pass and was intercepted. The Minnesota fans could hardly believe what happened next.

Fran Tarkenton faked a pass on the Colts' 4-yard line and ran the ball over himself. The Vikings won, 28-20.

Protection at last! Grady Alderman (67) gets in the way of a Pittsburgh defenseman as Fran searches for a receiver.

Colts Gino Marchetti *(89)* and Billy Ray Smith *(74)* put the fast rush on Fran for a 12-yard loss.

They wound up the 1961 season 3-10-0, in the Western Conference cellar. "Things could have been a lot worse," the Minnesota fans said cheerfully.

And they were—in 1962. During that season, the Vikings went 2-11-1. On one of Fran's really bad days, he was booed. It had never happened before. The fans yelled, "Get him out of there!"

Fran walked sadly to the sidelines. Veteran Hugh McElhenny put his arm around the rookie. He said:

"Well, kid, you've arrived! Welcome to the NFL! You are now a pro quarterback. You've been booed and replaced. Welcome to the club."

It wasn't all boos, of course. The Minnesota fans supported their team, even if it was still raw. There was plenty of cheering for Fran as he scrambled bravely out of the reach of giant linebackers. In 1963 the team won 5, lost 8, and tied one. They were learning fast and Coach Van Brocklin was pushing them hard.

The next season they went 8-5-1. In one game against the Giants, Fran scrambled 40 yards behind the line of scrimmage before passing for a 10-yard gain. After that, the nickname "The Scrambler" was his forever.

He felt that he was finally doing a good job as a pro quarterback. The Vikings tied for second place in the Western Conference and actually began to think about winning the title.

In a 1963 game, 49er Clark Miller (74) downs Fran. Vikings won this game, 24-20.

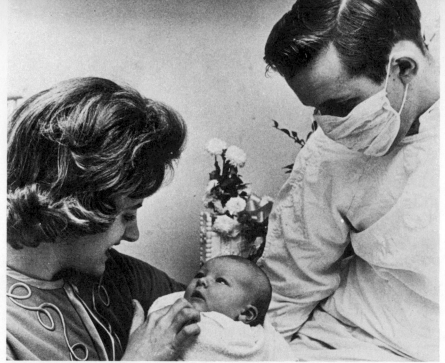
Fran and Elaine pose with their firstborn, Angela, in 1964.

Fran was now 24 years old. He and his wife had a new baby girl. They liked the friendly people of Minnesota. Fran had gone into business during the off-season and was doing well.

But a storm was brewing between Fran and Norm Van Brocklin. The coach was a man who often changed his mind. He had a fiery temper, too. He was under great pressure from the Viking owners to make the team a winner. So when Fran objected to some of the coach's decisions, bad feelings resulted.

Van Brocklin was also annoyed by Fran's scrambling. He, himself, had been an old-style "stand-up" quarterback. He wanted Fran to stay in the pocket of blockers.

But all too often in those days, when Fran needed the pocket the most, it wasn't there!

The 1965 season, which was supposed to bring the Vikings the title, turned out to be a disaster. They won seven and lost seven and finished fifth. Van Brocklin announced that he was quitting, then changed his mind.

But he was no longer able to inspire the team. In 1966 the Vikings went 4-9-1, sharing the Western Division cellar with the Detroit Lions.

During that sad season, Van Brocklin had benched Fran several times. The reasons given for this did not seem fair to Fran. Toward the end of 1966, Fran decided that he would ask to be traded. When he broke the news early the next year, Van Brocklin said he would quit, too.

Some people hoped this would make Fran decide to stay in Minnesota. But the Georgia quarterback's mind was made up. He was traded to the New York Giants.

Scrambling doesn't do much good when the Packer defense zeroes in on an unprotected quarterback.

Frustration shows on the faces of Fran, Coach Van Brocklin *(left)* and other Vikings as the Green Bay Packers demolish the team in a 1965 meeting.

Allie Sherman *(left)* coach of the New York Giants, shows his happiness as he introduces his new quarterback to the press in 1967. In the trade, New York gave up the first and second round draft choices for 1967, their number one draft for 1968 and another player to be agreed upon at a later date.

From 1958 through 1963, the Giants had won five conference titles. But they always lost the NFL championship. The fans loved them and hated them at the same time.

Then Coach Allie Sherman traded off some of his older stars. He gambled that he would be able to bring up younger players to take their place—and he lost.

The Giants dropped to seventh place in 1964. They pulled themselves up to second in 1965. But in 1966 they went 1-12-1. Yankee Stadium was filled with sobs, screams of fury, and fans singing "Good-bye, Allie" to the unfortunate coach.

Fran Tarkenton was the answer to Allie Sherman's prayer.

33

As quarterback, Fran knew he would have to do more than call plays. When he arrived in New York, he made it his business to meet and make friends with all his new teammates. All through the exhibition season, he studied the Giants, worked with them, and won their respect.

Then they went to St. Louis for the season opener against the Cardinals. The first time the Giants had possession, they went 76 yards for a touchdown. The Cardinals scored, too, and it was 10-7 in favor of St. Louis at the half.

Then Fran completed a 38-yard pass to Homer Jones, setting up a touchdown. The Cardinals fumbled and the Giants took advantage of it. Fran passed for three more touchdowns and the Giants won, 37-20.

Allie Sherman threw his arms around Fran's neck and cried.

Fran goes over strategy with Steve Wright and Homer Jones.

Fran gags it up in the Giants locker room. At left, Coach Alex Webster.

Next week, they faced a tougher rival, the Dallas Cowboys. The crafty Texans refused to blitz Fran. And throwing from the pocket, Fran was less than great. The Giants lost, 38-24.

Their next game, against Washington, saw them leading 34-32. Then Giant safety Carl Lockhart intercepted a pass in the end zone and fumbled. The ball was recovered by Washington and the Redskins went for the winning touchdown. It was a fluke, but it had robbed the Giants of victory.

They played their first home game in Yankee
Stadium against the New Orleans Saints. New York
scored early, but the Saints fought back. In the last
quarter, it was 21-20 with New Orleans in the lead.

Then Fran started a drive that took the Giants 69
yards. A roll-out pass to Bob Crespino in the end
zone brought the winning touchdown and a final score
of Giants 27, Saints 21.

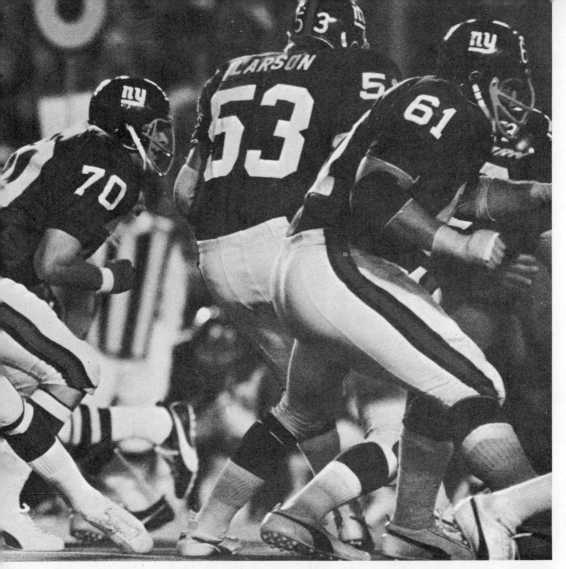

Fran with teammates Junior Coffey (34), Robert Hyland (70), Gregory Larson (53), and Charles Harper (61).

The 63,000 fans made Yankee Stadium rock with their cheers. Fran remembered a little boy with his bubble-gum cards who had dreamed of this moment.

It may not have been the whole world cheering him that day, but it sure seemed like it.

In the years that followed, Fran earned a solid place as one of the all-time great quarterbacks. He was unlucky, however, in playing for the Giants during a time of high hopes that were never fulfilled. The team came up from the cellar to third place in 1967 and second in 1968 and 1969. But not even the hiring of a new coach, Alex Webster, could put them in reach of an NFL title.

Meanwhile, the Minnesota Vikings under Coach Bud Grant had developed one of football's leading defenses. They won four straight Central Division championships and took the NFL title in 1969. But their offense was still weak.

The Giants, still trying to find a team that would click, talked about trading Fran Tarkenton in 1971. He said: "If you're going to trade me, I'd like to go back to Minnesota."

Fran relaxes with some young fans during the start of the 1973 exhibition season.

So Fran and his family made plans to move back to the land of evergreen trees and sky-blue waters. The Vikings had paid a high price for him, since he was now the fifth leading lifetime passer. Not only was he a football superstar, but he was also a successful businessman who had proved his ability to think for himself.

In 1972, he helped bring the Vikings to within two games of the NFL playoffs. But the Vikings' ancient foe, the Green Bay Packers, won the key game, 23-10.

"I'll get to the Super Bowl yet," said Fran with a smile. "Even if I have to scramble all the way."

Fran scoots for a quick touch down in this 1973 game with the Chicago Bears.

It had taken all of 1972 for Fran and the Vikings to learn to work together again. But when 1973 began, everybody could see that the Viking offense finally cooked. Minnesota won 10 games in a row.

The Vikes clinched the Central Division title. They finished with a 12-2 record. Much of the credit went to Fran, who helped Coach Grant's dreams of glory by throwing 169 completions for 2,113 yards. His interception percentage was a stingy 2.6.

The Vikings won their first playoff against the Washington Redskins. Then they faced the Dallas Cowboys for the NFC Championship.

Action from the 1973 Conference Title game against the Dallas Cowboys.

The Vikings led by only 10-7 in the third quarter of that game. Then Fran uncorked a 54-yard bomb. It soared toward wide receiver John Gilliam. Cowboy cornerback Mel Renfro almost managed to haul the ball down. But not quite. Gilliam scooped it in. Touchdown! Minnesota's lead widened to 17-7—and after that, they were off to the races.

The playoff ended with a 27-10 Viking victory. And a ticket to Super Bowl VIII. It was the second trip for Minnesota, which had lost Super Bowl IV to the Kansas City Chiefs.

But it was the first Super Bowl for Fran.

41

The Vikes' opponent was the Miami Dolphins. Miami had won Super Bowl VII. They had a great scrambling quarterback in Bob Griese and a human tank in running back Larry Csonka. The Miami defense was legendary. The Viking defense allowed just 168 points in 1973. But they were second-best. Tops was Miami, which allowed only 150.

At the start of Super Bowl VIII, Minnesota got a hint of the kind of day it was going to be.

Miami had the ball first. Griese fed the ball to fleet Mercury Morris and to Csonka. The team marched along. Griese passed only twice, but got good gains each time. And after only 5 minutes had ticked by, Miami had a touchdown.

Minnesota took over. And the poor Vikes didn't even get a first down.

Miami's next series was nearly a carbon-copy of the first. Ten plays in five minutes equals one touchdown. Miami 14, Minnesota 0.

In the second quarter, Garo Yepremian kicked a field goal for the Dolphins and it was 17-0. Despite all that Fran could do, the score stayed that way into the middle of the third quarter. Minnesota could not move.

Miami scored again and it was 24-0. In the last period, Fran fired pass after pass. Then he ran the ball into the end zone himself for a touchdown! But it was a futile try. Minnesota was whipped, 24-7.

Fran breaks through for a touchdown during Super Bowl VIII (1973)

Fran was bitterly disappointed. But he had done his best. And even during the off-season, he had little time to brood. For Fran Tarkenton was more than a football player—he was also a businessman.

He believed that pro athletes had to do more than play their game. A football career didn't last forever. One day, the cheering would stop and he would have to earn a living at something else. So Fran had a new business of his own. It helped companies get the best out of their workers by motivating them to do their best.

Fran's company aced as a kind of "super coach" to other businesses.

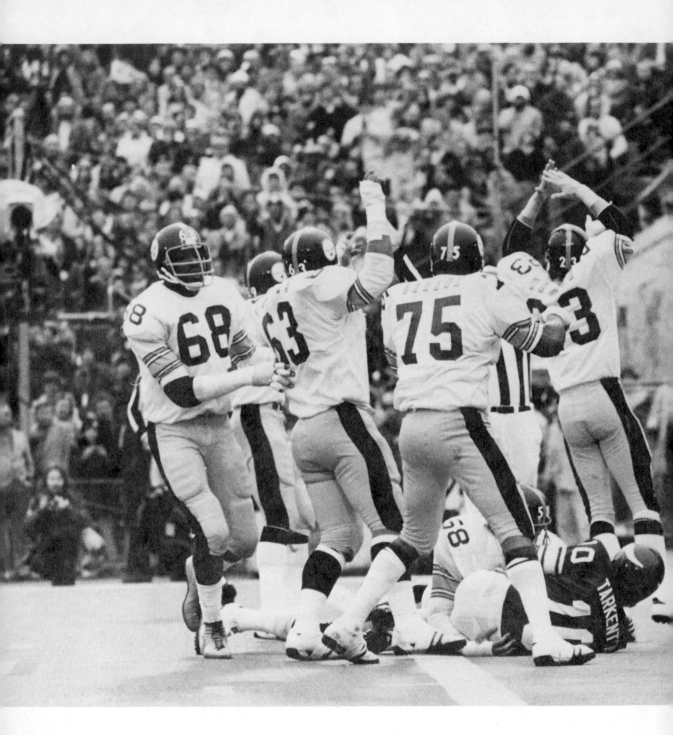

In 1974, the Vikings were 10-4. They defeated St. Louis in the first round of the playoffs, then beat Los Angeles, 10-14, for the Conference title.

Then it was time for Minnesota's third Super Bowl bid—against the upstart Pittsburgh Steelers. The first half saw only a single score. There was Fran Tarkenton in the end zone with the ball. . . .

But it was the *Minnesota* end zone! And the score was 2 points for the Steelers on a safety. In the second half, a Minnesota fumble set up a Steeler TD. The Vikes got a 6-pointer in the last period. But then the Steelers marched 66 yards and wrapped it up, 16-6.

The 1975 season was destined to be a landmark one for Fran. He topped Johnny Unitas in lifetime TD passes and completions. Fran was now a 15-year veteran. Bud Grant said of him:

"Fran Tarkenton fits perfectly the adage that the longer you play quarterback, the better you get."

He was the No. 1 NFL passer of all time, with 5,225 attempts, 2,931 completions, a 56.1 percentage. Thanks to his scrambling, he was also No. 1 quarterback rusher!

The Vikings were 12-2. They went to the playoffs against Dallas sure that they would win. But Dallas eked out a 17-14 victory with a touchdown in the last 24 seconds of the game.

Almost the entire Pittsburg Defense surrounds Fran as they catch him in the end zone for a safety during Super Bowl IX

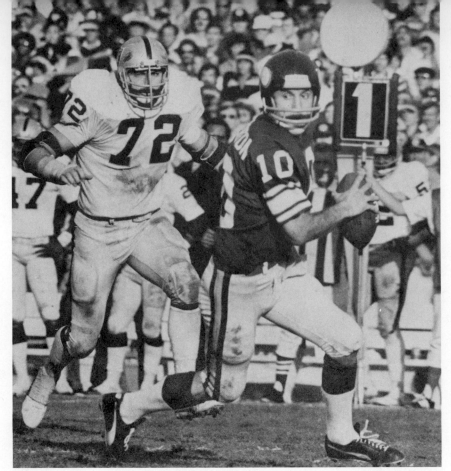
The Oakland Raiders defense was all over Fran during Super Bowl XI (1977)

During the 1976 season, Fran piled numbers onto his NFL passing records. He broke Johnny Unitas' yardage record with a new total of 41,801. The team was 11-2-1. Playoff wins against the Washington Redskins and the Los Angeles Rams sent the Vikings to the Super Bowl for the fourth time. This time Minnesota faced the Oakland Raiders, who had lost Super Bowl II to Vince Lombardi's Packers.

Somebody asked Viking Coach Bud Grant what advantages his team would have in Super Bowl XI. "We have more experience," he said with a grin.

The Raiders were super-tough and super-hungry. For nine miserable years, they had been trying to escape from the playoffs alive. And now they had made it.

Nothing could stop Oakland in Super Bowl XI. Minnesota made mistakes—and the Raiders were always ready to take advantage. Fran threw his first-ever Super Bowl TD pass. But he also suffered an interception that Raider Willie Brown ran 75 yards for a touchdown. When the last gun sounded, it was Oakland 32, Minnesota 14.

The Vikings took defeat calmly. "We'll be back," said Coach Bud Grant.

And Fran Tarkenton added with a grin: "We're just going to have to find an AFC team we can beat!"

FRANCIS ASBURY TARKENTON

He was born in Richmond, Virginia, on February 3, 1940. His father named him after Francis Asbury, pioneer Methodist missionary in the United States.

Fran graduated from Athens High School in Georgia in 1957. He attended the University of Georgia from 1957-1961 and married Elaine Merrell on December 22, 1960. The couple has three children.

Fran Tarkenton played for the Minnesota Vikings from 1961 through 1966, and for the New York Giants from 1967 through 1971. In 1972 he rejoined the Vikings. He is a wealthy man from real estate and stock investments as well as from his salary, one of the highest in pro football. He has written about his life in *Better Scramble Than Lose* (1969); *Broken Patterns: The Education of a Quarterback* (1971) and *Tarkenton* (1976).

	Team	Passes Att.	Comp.	Pct.	Yds.	TD	Int.
1961	Vikings	280	157	.56	1,997	18	17
1962	Vikings	329	163	.49	2,595	22	25
1963	Vikings	297	170	.57	2,311	15	15
1964	Vikings	306	171	.56	2,506	22	11
1965	Vikings	329	171	.52	2,609	19	11
1966	Vikings	358	192	.54	2,561	17	16
1967	Giants	377	204	.54	3,088	29	19
1968	Giants	337	182	.54	2,555	21	12
1969	Giants	409	220	.54	2,918	23	8
1970	Giants	389	219	.56	2,777	19	12
1971	Giants	386	226	.59	2,567	11	21
1972	Vikings	378	215	.57	2,651	18	13
1973	Vikings	274	169	.62	2,113	15	7
1974	Vikings	351	199	.57	2,598	17	12
1975	Vikings	425	273	.64	2,994	25	13
1976	Vikings	412	255	61.9	2,961	17	8
TOTALS		5,637	3,186	57	41,801	308	220